Parenting
in the Digital Age

A Practical Guide to Raising Teens in the Social Media World

ZARA WOODS

Copyright

© 2024, **Zara Woods**

All rights reserved.

No part of this book may be reproduced, distributed, or transmitted in any form or by any means, including photocopying, recording, or other electronic or mechanical methods, without the prior written permission of the author, except in the case of brief quotations embodied in critical reviews and certain other noncommercial uses permitted by copyright law.

Disclaimer

The information contained in this book is for general informational purposes only. The author, Zara Woods assumes no responsibility for errors or omissions in the contents of the book. While the author has made every effort to ensure that the information in this book was correct at the time of publication, the author does not warrant the accuracy, completeness, or usefulness of any information provided. The reader should not rely solely on the information within this book for their specific needs and should seek professional advice where appropriate. The author disclaims any liability, loss, or risk, personal or otherwise, which is incurred as a consequence, directly or indirectly, of the use and application of any of the contents of this any of the contents of this book.

COPYRIGHT	2
DISCLAIMER	3
INTRODUCTION	7
UNDERSTANDING THE DIGITAL WORLD TEENS LIVE IN	**7**
Why This Guide is Important for Modern Parenting	8
How to Use This Book Effectively	10
Final Thoughts	12
CHAPTER 1:	**15**
THE DIGITAL AGE DEMYSTIFIED	**15**
The Evolution of Social Media: From Past to Present	16
The Role of Technology in Teen Lives: Benefits and Challenges	19
The Psychological Impact of Social Media on Teens	23
Bridging the Digital Generation Gap: Understanding and Connection	25
CHAPTER 2:	**29**
EXPLORING SOCIAL MEDIA PLATFORMS	**29**
Overview of Popular Social Media	30
Platforms	30
Positive Aspects of Social Media: Creativity, Learning, and Connection	37
Risks and Dangers of Social Media: What Parents Should Know	39
CHAPTER 3:	**43**
BUILDING HEALTHY DIGITAL HABITS	**43**
Setting Screen Time Boundaries: Finding Balance	44
Promoting Positive Online Behavior: Respect and Responsibility	47
Developing Digital Literacy: Critical Thinking Skills	50
Fostering Real-World Connections: Balancing Online and Offline Life	53
CHAPTER 4:	**59**
PRIVACY AND SAFETY IN THE DIGITAL SPACE	**59**
Understanding and Setting Privacy Controls	60
Protecting Personal Information: What Teens Need to Know	62
Safeguarding Against Online Predators and Scams	64
Basic Cybersecurity: Keeping Devices and Data Secure	67

CHAPTER 5: 71
MENTAL HEALTH AND SOCIAL MEDIA 71

- Recognizing Signs of Social Media-Induced Anxiety and Depression 72
- Addressing Body Image and Self-Esteem Challenges 74
- The Impact of Online Validation and Dopamine Loops 76
- When to Seek Professional Help: Support Resources 79

CHAPTER 6: 83
EFFECTIVE COMMUNICATION WITH YOUR TEEN 83

- Initiating Conversations: How to Talk About Social Media 84
- Active Listening: Understanding Your Teen's Perspective 86
- Conflict Resolution: Handling Disagreements Constructively 89
- Building Trust: Creating Open Dialogue About Online Activities 91

CHAPTER 7: 95
FOSTERING POSITIVE DIGITAL CITIZENSHIP 95

- Teaching Empathy and Respect in Online Interactions 96
- Encouraging Authenticity: Being True to Oneself Online 98
- Using Social Media for Good: Promoting Positive Causes 100
- Leading by Example: How Your Social Media Habits Influence Your Teen 102

CHAPTER 8: 107
MANAGING SOCIAL MEDIA THROUGH LIFE TRANSITIONS 107

- Balancing Academics and Social Media: Strategies for Success 108
- Exploring Social Changes: Friendships and Relationships 110
- Supporting Teens Through Online Challenges: Breakups, Rumors, and More 113
- Preparing for the Future: Social Media and College Admissions 116

CHAPTER 9: 121
PARENTING STRATEGIES FOR THE DIGITAL FUTURE 121

- Staying Ahead: Emerging Social Media Trends 122
- Preparing Teens for a Digital Career: Skills and Opportunities 124
- Lifelong Digital Literacy: Cultivating Future Skills 127
- Adapting to Technological Changes: Continuous Learning 130

CHAPTER 10: 135

TOOLS, RESOURCES, AND SUPPORT FOR PARENTS **135**
    APPS AND TOOLS FOR MONITORING AND MANAGING SOCIAL MEDIA USE 135
    SAMPLE FAMILY MEDIA AGREEMENTS: SETTING CLEAR EXPECTATIONS 140
    - TOPICS TO INCLUDE: 141
    MENTAL HEALTH AND SUPPORT RESOURCES: WHERE TO GET
    HELP 143
    - MENTAL HEALTH SUPPORT 143

CONCLUSION: **147**
EMPOWERING PARENTS AND TEENS IN THE DIGITAL WORLD **147**
    RECAP: SUPPORTING HEALTHY DIGITAL HABITS AND STRONG
    RELATIONSHIPS 148
    ENCOURAGING GROWTH AND INDEPENDENCE IN THE DIGITAL
    AGE 151
    MOVING FORWARD: CONTINUAL LEARNING AND ADAPTATION
    152

Introduction

Understanding the Digital World Teens Live In

Today's teenagers spend hours every day connected to devices that give them access to an almost unlimited amount of information, entertainment, and social interaction. This digital world is their reality.

Social media, in particular, plays a big role in how they develop their sense of identity, form relationships, and interact with the world around them.

For parents, understanding this digital environment is key—not just to guide teens but also to help them navigate it safely and responsibly.

Unlike previous generations, today's teens are digital natives, having grown up with the internet as a constant presence in their lives. They don't just use technology; they live within it. From chatting with friends on Instagram to creating videos on TikTok, their online experiences are deeply embedded in their daily routines. But along with these opportunities come challenges that can be difficult to manage, especially for parents who grew up in a world where social media didn't exist.

Why This Guide is Important for Modern Parenting

This guide is here to help parents understand the digital world that their teens are so immersed in.

While the fundamentals of parenting remain the same, the strategies we use need to adapt to address the realities of the digital age. The decisions you make as a parent regarding your teen's online activities can have long-lasting effects on their mental health, social development, and future opportunities.

Why is this guide important?

Because the digital world is complex, it has the potential to offer incredible opportunities, but it also poses significant risks. On the positive side, social media can be a platform for creativity, connection, and learning. On the negative side, it can expose teens to cyberbullying, addiction, and harmful content. This book aims to help you understand these dual realities and provides practical tools and advice to support your teen effectively.

What makes this guide different is its practical approach. We're not just discussing theories or giving vague advice. You'll find specific strategies, real-world examples, and actionable tips that you can start using right away. Whether your concern is about too much screen time, the dangers of online predators, or simply trying to understand the latest trends on TikTok, this book offers clear guidance.

How to Use This Book Effectively

You don't need to be a tech expert to guide your teen through the digital age. What you do need is an open mind, a willingness to learn, and a commitment to keeping communication open with your teen. This book is structured to help you do just that, breaking down the complexities of the digital world into easy-to-understand sections.

Here's how to make the most of this guide:

- *Start Where You Need It Most:* You don't have to read this book from start to finish. Each chapter is designed to stand alone, so feel free to jump to the sections that address your immediate concerns.

- *Engage in Conversations:* Use the information in this book to start meaningful conversations with your teen. Throughout the chapters, you'll find suggestions for how to talk about difficult topics in a way that encourages open dialogue.

- *Apply the Strategies:* Every chapter includes practical steps you can take to address specific issues. Whether it's setting up privacy controls, establishing screen time rules, or helping your teen take a break from social media, you'll find actionable advice that you can start using right away.

- *Reflect and Adapt*: The digital world is always changing, and so should your approach to it. Regularly revisit the strategies in this book and be open to adapting them as your teen grows and as new technologies emerge.

This book is designed to be a resource you can return to as needed, whether you're trying to understand the basics of social media or dealing with more complex issues like online bullying. By the time you finish this guide, you'll have a clearer understanding of the digital world your teen is living in and the confidence to help them scale it safely and responsibly.

Final Thoughts

Parenting in the digital age is not about eliminating all risks, it's about managing them and helping your teen make informed, responsible choices. It's about being proactive rather than reactive, and about building a relationship with your teen based on trust and communication. As you move forward, remember that you're not alone. Many parents are facing the same challenges, and with the right tools and mindset, you can help your teen thrive both online and offline.

From understanding how social media has evolved to building healthy digital habits, this book will give you the knowledge and strategies you need to raise a confident, connected, and responsible teen in today's fast-changing world.

Chapter 1:

The Digital Age Demystified

Analyzing the world of social media and digital technology, it's crucial to first understand the landscape that our teens are passing through every day. The digital age has brought about unprecedented changes in how we communicate, learn, and interact with one another.

For teens, who are growing up in this environment, these platforms are more than just tools—they are integral parts of their lives. This chapter will guide you through the evolution of social media, the role of technology in your teen's life, the psychological impacts of these platforms, and how to bridge the generational gap in understanding these changes.

The Evolution of Social Media: From Past to Present

Social media has undergone a remarkable transformation over the past two decades. What began as simple online communication tools has evolved into complex ecosystems that significantly influence culture, identity, and even global events.

- *The Early Days: MySpace and Friendster*: The journey of social media began in the early 2000s with platforms like MySpace and Friendster. These sites were pioneers in the concept of online social networking. They allowed users to create profiles, connect with friends, and share content such as photos and status updates. The focus was on building digital representations of oneself, which laid the groundwork for the social media explosion that would follow.

- *Facebook's Impact*: In 2004, Facebook changed the game. Unlike its predecessors, Facebook emphasized real-world identity verification, encouraging users to connect with their actual friends and family. This shift towards authenticity was pivotal, as it transformed social media from a space of anonymous interactions to a platform where real-life connections could be maintained and nurtured. Facebook's introduction of the News Feed further personalized user experiences, curating content based on interactions and preferences—a feature that became a standard across other platforms.

- *The Rise of Visual Content*: By the 2010s, visual content became the focal point of social media, driven by platforms like Instagram and Pinterest. Instagram, in particular, revolutionized the way people shared their lives online, focusing on high-quality visuals and the concept of "likes" as social currency. This visual appeal attracted a younger audience, leading to Instagram's rapid growth among teens who were eager to express themselves through images.

- *TikTok and the Era of Short-Form Content*: Today, TikTok represents the latest evolution in social media. Launched in 2016, TikTok capitalized on the trend towards shorter, more engaging content. It allows users to create and share 15-60 second videos, often set to music, making it a hub for creativity, trends, and viral challenges. TikTok's algorithm is designed to keep users engaged for as long as possible, learning from their behavior to show them increasingly tailored content. This shift towards short-form content reflects the changing attention spans and preferences of today's digital natives.

- *The Future of Social Media*: Looking ahead, social media is poised to continue its evolution with emerging technologies such as augmented reality (AR) and virtual reality (VR). These advancements promise to make online interactions even more immersive, raising new questions about privacy, identity, and the impact of virtual experiences on real-world behavior. As parents, staying informed about these developments will be crucial in guiding your teens through the digital landscape.

The Role of Technology in Teen Lives: Benefits and Challenges

For today's teens, technology is an integral part of their daily lives. It shapes how they learn, socialize, and even how they perceive themselves. Understanding the dual role that technology plays—the opportunities it offers and the challenges it poses—is essential for effective parenting in the digital age.

- ***Opportunities:***
  - Learning and Education: The internet has opened up new avenues for learning. Educational platforms

like Khan Academy, Coursera, and even YouTube provide access to a vast array of information on virtually any topic. Teens can take courses, watch tutorials, and engage with educational content that supplements what they learn in school. This has made learning more accessible and personalized, allowing students to explore subjects at their own pace.

- *Creativity and Self-Expression*: Social media platforms provide teens with a stage to express their creativity. Whether through photography on Instagram, video creation on TikTok, or writing on blogs, these platforms offer opportunities to explore and develop their creative talents. For example, many young artists have gained recognition and even career opportunities by showcasing their work online. Social media serves as a modern-day portfolio where creativity is not just shared but celebrated.

- *Social Connection*: Social media allows teens to stay connected with their peers and family, regardless of physical distance. This has been particularly important during the COVID-19 pandemic, where social media became a lifeline for maintaining relationships and a sense of normalcy.

It also provides spaces where teens can find communities that share their interests or experiences, such as LGBTQ+ groups, gaming communities, or fan clubs. These connections can provide much-needed support and a sense of belonging.

- *Challenges:*

- *Distraction and Addiction*: The design of social media platforms, with features like infinite scrolling and personalized content feeds, is intended to maximize user engagement. This can lead to addiction, where teens feel compelled to check their accounts constantly, even at the expense of sleep, homework, or face-to-face interactions. The constant bombardment of notifications and the pressure to stay updated with the latest trends can also create a significant distraction from real-world responsibilities.

- *Cyberbullying and Peer Pressure*: The anonymity and distance provided by the internet can sometimes lead to harmful behavior. Cyberbullying is a significant issue, with teens sometimes using social media to spread rumors, exclude others, or post derogatory comments. Peer pressure is also amplified online, where the number of likes, comments, and followers can become a measure of popularity or self-worth. The public nature of social media means that these interactions are often visible to a wider audience, which can intensify the emotional impact.

- *Privacy Concerns*: Teens often share more information online than they realize, from personal details to their location. This can expose them to risks like identity theft, stalking, or exploitation. Moreover, once something is shared online, it's challenging to remove it completely, leading to potential long-term consequences. Educating teens about the importance of privacy settings and the potential dangers of oversharing is crucial in protecting their digital footprint.

The Psychological Impact of Social Media on Teens

Social media's impact on teen psychology is profound. While it can offer a sense of belonging and self-expression, it can also lead to significant mental health challenges.

- *Self-Esteem and Body Image*: Social media often presents an idealized version of reality, where users curate their lives to show only the most appealing aspects. This constant exposure to perfection—

whether it's in terms of physical appearance, lifestyle, or achievements—can lead to feelings of inadequacy among teens. They may start to compare themselves unfavorably to others, leading to lower self-esteem and body image issues. For instance, the prevalence of edited and filtered images on platforms like Instagram can create unrealistic beauty standards that are impossible to achieve.

- *Social Anxiety and FOMO (Fear of Missing Out)*: The ability to see what others are doing at all times can exacerbate feelings of social anxiety. If a teen sees their friends hanging out without them, it can lead to feelings of exclusion and loneliness, often referred to as FOMO. This can cause them to feel like they are missing out on important social experiences, leading to increased anxiety and a compulsive need to stay connected online.

- *The Need for Validation*: Social media metrics—likes, comments, shares—become a form of social validation. Teens may start to tie their self-worth to how much engagement their posts receive, leading to a cycle where their mood and self-esteem are dependent on their social media interactions. This can also create pressure to post content that they believe will attract more attention, sometimes at the cost of authenticity or comfort.

Bridging the Digital Generation Gap: Understanding and Connection

The digital generation gap is one of the most significant challenges for parents today. The world in which today's teens are growing up is vastly different from the one their parents knew at the same age. Bridging this gap requires understanding, patience, and a willingness to learn.

- *Start with Curiosity*, Not Judgment: Instead of immediately criticizing your teen's social media use, try to approach it with curiosity. Ask them to explain what they enjoy about certain platforms and why they follow specific trends or influencers. This approach not only helps you understand their online world better but also opens up lines of communication that can be essential when addressing more serious issues.

- *Learn Together*: Technology evolves rapidly, and it can be challenging to keep up with the latest trends, platforms, and slang. Consider learning about new technologies and social media trends alongside your teen. This could involve researching new apps, watching YouTube videos together, or even trying out a platform like TikTok yourself. By engaging with the digital world on their terms, you can build a stronger bond and demonstrate that you're invested in understanding their experiences.

- *Share Your Experiences*: Although the technology may be different, the fundamental challenges of growing up—such as dealing with peer pressure, forming an identity, and navigating friendships—remain the same. Sharing your experiences and how you handled similar situations can provide valuable context and guidance for your teen. It also helps them see that you understand their struggles, even if the medium has changed.

- *Set Reasonable Boundaries*: Establishing rules and boundaries around social media use is essential, but these should be done collaboratively. Involve your teen in setting these boundaries, so they understand the reasoning behind them and feel a sense of ownership. For example, you might agree on no phone use during family meals or setting specific times for screen-free activities. The key is to create guidelines that balance safety and freedom, allowing your teen to enjoy social media without letting it dominate their life.

The digital age has transformed the way we live, particularly for teenagers who are growing up with social media as a central part of their lives. Understanding the evolution of social media, the role of technology in your teen's life, and the psychological impact these platforms can have is crucial for guiding them effectively. By bridging the digital generation gap, you can build a stronger relationship with your teen and help them navigate the complexities of the digital world with confidence and responsibility.

Chapter 2:

Exploring Social Media Platforms

As a parent, understanding the various social media platforms your teen engages with is essential for guiding them safely through the digital world. Each platform comes with its own unique features, culture, and potential risks. Whether your teen is using Instagram to share photos, TikTok to create videos, or Snapchat to connect with friends, these platforms play a significant role in how they communicate, express themselves, and interact with others.

This chapter will provide a comprehensive overview of the most popular platforms, the appeal they hold for teens, and the potential dangers they pose. By gaining a deeper understanding of these platforms, you'll be better equipped to help your teen navigate them responsibly.

Overview of Popular Social Media Platforms

Each social media platform offers something unique, and teens are often drawn to different ones depending on their interests and social circles. Below is a breakdown of the most widely used platforms and what makes them so appealing to teens.

- *Instagram*:

- Focus: Instagram is a visually-driven platform where users share photos, videos, and stories with their followers. It's particularly popular among teens for its emphasis on aesthetics and the ability to curate a personal brand or image.

- *Why Teens Love It*: Instagram allows teens to showcase their lives, interests, and social circles through carefully selected photos and videos. The "like" system provides instant feedback, which can be both gratifying and anxiety-inducing.

- *Key Features:* Instagram's main features include posts, Stories (which disappear after 24 hours), IGTV for longer videos, and Reels for short, entertaining clips. It also has a private messaging system (DMs) that teens often use for one-on-one conversations.

- *Risks*: Instagram can foster unhealthy comparisons and body image issues, as users tend to share idealized versions of their lives. The platform also has a history of cyberbullying and privacy concerns. Teens may also feel pressured to gain likes, followers, and attention, sometimes at the expense of their well-being.

- ***TikTok:***

- *Focus*: TikTok is all about short-form video content. It's known for its fast-paced, engaging videos, often set to music, and has quickly become a favorite among teens for its creativity and viral trends.

- *Why Teens Love It:* TikTok encourages creativity, with its easy-to-use video editing tools and wide variety of music, effects, and challenges. The platform is also highly addictive, with its algorithm showing users a never-ending stream of content tailored to their interests.

- *Key Features*: TikTok's "For You" page offers personalized content, and users can create videos up to three minutes long. Teens often participate in viral trends, challenges, or dances, which can quickly amass likes and views.

- *Risks:* The addictive nature of TikTok can lead to excessive screen time. Additionally, its algorithm can expose teens to inappropriate or harmful content, and the pressure to go viral can push them to engage in risky behaviors or challenges. Cyberbullying and privacy are also concerns, especially with the ability to interact with strangers.

- ***Snapchat:***

   - *Focus:* Snapchat is designed for quick, temporary communication. Its key feature is that messages and content disappear after being viewed, creating a sense of privacy and exclusivity.

   - *Why Teens Love It:* Teens enjoy the temporary nature of Snapchat because it feels less permanent and judgmental than other platforms. It encourages playful interaction with its filters, lenses, and Bitmoji avatars.

- *Key Features*: Snapchat's Stories allow users to share content with their followers for 24 hours, while Snaps (photos or videos) disappear after being viewed. Other features include private messaging, Snap Map (which shows users' locations), and Streaks, which track consecutive days of messaging between users.

- *Risks:* The disappearing content can lead to impulsive behavior, with teens feeling that what they post is consequence-free. However, content can still be captured via screenshots. The Snap Map feature also raises privacy concerns, as it reveals real-time location data. Cyberbullying and the sharing of explicit content are additional risks.

- **YouTube:**
  - *Focus*: YouTube is a video-sharing platform that hosts everything from educational content to entertainment. It's a place where teens can follow their favorite creators or upload their own videos.

- *Why Teens Love It*: YouTube provides endless entertainment and learning opportunities. Teens follow influencers, tutorials, gaming channels, and more. It's also a creative outlet for teens who want to share their own content.

- *Key Features*: Users can subscribe to channels, like and comment on videos, and upload their own content. YouTube's recommendation algorithm suggests videos based on users' viewing history, making it easy to fall into hours of video consumption.

- *Risks:* While YouTube offers valuable content, it also exposes teens to inappropriate or harmful material. The comments section can be a breeding ground for negativity and cyberbullying. Additionally, many influencers promote materialism or unhealthy behaviors, which can affect teens' self-image and choices.

- **_Twitter:_**

- *Focus:* Twitter is a platform for sharing short updates, thoughts, and news in the form of tweets, which are limited to 280 characters.

- *Why Teens Love It:* Teens use Twitter to keep up with current events, follow celebrities and influencers, and share their thoughts in real-time. Its fast-paced nature makes it appealing for engaging in conversations or trending topics.

- *Key Features:* Tweets can include text, images, or links. Users can retweet, reply, or like content, and trending topics help guide discussions. Teens also use Twitter's private messaging system (DMs) to communicate more privately.

- *Risks:* Twitter's open format exposes teens to a wide range of content, including potentially harmful material or toxic discussions. Cyberbullying and harassment are common due to the platform's anonymity. Teens might also feel pressure to engage in trending topics or heated debates, which can lead to emotional distress.

Positive Aspects of Social Media: Creativity, Learning, and Connection

While there are notable risks, it's important to recognize that social media also offers valuable opportunities for teens. These platforms can be powerful tools for creativity, learning, and social connection when used mindfully.

- *Creativity and Self-Expression:* Platforms like Instagram, TikTok, and YouTube give teens the freedom to explore their creative talents. Whether through photography, video production, music, or graphic design, social media provides an outlet for self-expression that can boost confidence and help teens find their voice. Teens can also receive feedback from their peers, which, when positive, can encourage further development of their skills.

- *Learning and Educational Resources*: YouTube and TikTok, among others, host a wealth of educational content. Teens can learn new skills, explore academic interests, or even prepare for exams using these platforms. Many educators and creators share free, high-quality content that can supplement what teens are learning in school. From DIY tutorials to coding lessons, social media has become a valuable resource for self-directed learning.

- *Social Connection*: Social media allows teens to stay in touch with their friends and make new connections. During periods of isolation, like the COVID-19 pandemic, social media became an essential tool for maintaining friendships and a sense of community. Online groups and fan communities provide spaces where teens can bond over shared interests, whether it's a favorite band, video game, or social cause.

Risks and Dangers of Social Media: What Parents Should Know

While the benefits are significant, the risks associated with social media use should not be overlooked. It's important to be aware of the potential dangers and how to mitigate them.

- *Cyberbullying:* Cyberbullying is one of the most serious concerns for teens using social media. The anonymity and distance provided by these platforms can encourage mean-spirited behavior. Teens may use social media to spread rumors, send hurtful messages, or publicly shame their peers. The effects of cyberbullying can be devastating, leading to anxiety, depression, and even suicidal thoughts. Parents should be vigilant for signs of bullying, such as sudden changes in mood, withdrawal from social interactions, or reluctance to use social media.

- *Social Media Addiction:* The design of social media platforms, with their endless scrolling and frequent notifications, is meant to keep users engaged for as long as possible. For teens, this can lead to social media addiction, where they feel the need to constantly check their accounts. This can interfere with their daily lives, leading to poor academic performance, sleep deprivation, and reduced face-to-face interactions. Establishing screen time limits and encouraging offline activities can help prevent addiction.

- *Peer Pressure and FOMO*: Social media amplifies peer pressure by allowing teens to see what their friends are doing at all times. If they feel left out of social events or experiences, they may develop a fear of missing out (FOMO), which can cause anxiety and negatively impact their self-esteem. This pressure can also lead teens to engage in risky behaviors, such as participating in viral challenges or sharing inappropriate content in an attempt to fit in or gain approval.

- *Privacy and Security Risks*: Teens often don't realize how much personal information they're sharing online. From location data to personal photos, everything they post can be accessed by others. This can make them vulnerable to identity theft, stalking, or online predators. It's essential to educate teens about the importance of privacy settings and to regularly review their accounts to ensure they're not oversharing. Social media plays a central role in the lives of today's teens, offering both opportunities for growth and exploration.

Chapter 3:

Building Healthy Digital Habits

As social media continues to permeate every aspect of daily life, particularly for teenagers, cultivating healthy digital habits is more important than ever. These habits not only ensure that social media remains a positive influence but also help mitigate the risks of addiction, mental health issues, and the erosion of real-world connections.

This chapter looks deep into practical strategies for setting boundaries, promoting responsible online behavior, and balancing screen time with offline activities. By establishing these habits early on, you can help your teen develop a healthier relationship with technology that will benefit them for years to come.

Setting Screen Time Boundaries: Finding Balance

In today's world, screens are ubiquitous, and finding the right balance between online and offline life is crucial for your teen's well-being. Setting screen time boundaries isn't just about limiting usage; it's about creating a structure that allows your teen to benefit from digital experiences while maintaining a healthy, active lifestyle.

- *Assessing Current Screen Time:* The first step in setting screen time boundaries is understanding how much time your teen currently spends on their devices and what they're doing during that time. Most smartphones have built-in screen time tracking tools that can help you get a clear picture. Look for patterns in their usage—are they engaging in educational activities, connecting with friends, or just mindlessly scrolling through social media? This assessment helps identify where adjustments are needed and sets the foundation for healthier habits.

- *Involving Your Teen in the Process:* Involving your teen in the process of setting screen time limits is crucial for ensuring their cooperation and understanding. Discuss the reasons why these boundaries are important, such as the impact on sleep, academic performance, and mental health. Work together to establish guidelines that everyone can agree on, such as no phones at the dinner table or limiting screen time before bed. When teens feel they have a say in the rules, they are more likely to respect them.

- *Creating Digital-Free Zones*: Designating certain areas of your home as screen-free zones can help reinforce the boundaries you set. For example, the dining room might be a place for conversation and eating, not for phones or tablets. Similarly, keeping the bedroom screen-free can promote better sleep hygiene by reducing the temptation to scroll late at night. These zones encourage more meaningful, offline interactions and help your teen disconnect from their devices.

- *Balancing Screen Time with Offline Activities*: Encouraging your teen to balance their screen time with offline activities is essential for their overall well-being. This can include physical exercise, hobbies, spending time with family, or engaging in face-to-face social interactions. The goal is to ensure that screen time doesn't crowd out other important aspects of life. Encourage your teen to pursue interests that don't involve screens, such as playing a musical instrument, reading, or participating in sports. These activities provide a healthy contrast to the digital world and contribute to their personal growth.

- *Regularly Revisiting and Adjusting Boundaries:* The digital world is constantly changing, and so are your teen's needs and habits. Regularly revisit the screen time rules to see how they're working. Are the boundaries being respected? Is your teen struggling with the limits? Use these check-ins as an opportunity to adjust the rules as needed and to reinforce the importance of maintaining a healthy balance. Flexibility is key—what works during the school year might need to be adjusted during holidays or summer break.

Promoting Positive Online Behavior: Respect and Responsibility

Teaching teens how to behave responsibly and respectfully online is just as important as managing how much time they spend there. Digital etiquette and ethics play a significant role in shaping the online environment, and helping your teen navigate these expectations is key to their safety and well-being.

- *Understanding Digital Citizenship:* Introduce your teen to the concept of digital citizenship, which involves being a responsible, respectful, and ethical participant in online communities. This includes understanding the impact of their actions online, respecting others' privacy, and being mindful of the digital footprint they leave behind. Digital citizenship also involves recognizing and reporting inappropriate behavior, whether it's cyberbullying, hate speech, or the spread of misinformation.

- *Encouraging Authenticity:* Social media often presents an idealized version of life, which can pressure teens to conform to unrealistic standards. Encourage your teen to be authentic in their online presence, sharing content that reflects who they are rather than what they think others want to see. Authenticity helps build self-confidence and reduces the stress associated with maintaining a curated image. Discuss the difference between sharing personal achievements and oversharing details that could compromise their privacy or safety.

- *Addressing Cyberbullying:* Make sure your teen understands what cyberbullying is and the harm it can cause. Discuss the importance of speaking out against bullying and not participating in harmful behavior. Equip your teen with strategies to deal with cyberbullying, such as blocking or reporting users who engage in such behavior, and encourage them to talk to you or another trusted adult if they encounter issues online. Reinforce the idea that kindness and respect should guide all of their online interactions.

- *The Power of Words:* Help your teen understand that words have power, even in the digital world. What may seem like a harmless joke or comment can have serious consequences for others. Encourage them to think before they post, to consider how their words might be interpreted, and to choose kindness over negativity. This awareness not only protects others but also helps your teen build a positive online reputation.

- *Promoting Empathy Online*: Encourage your teen to use social media as a platform for spreading positivity and supporting others. This could involve engaging with causes they care about, offering words of encouragement to friends, or simply being a positive influence in their online communities. Empathy online is just as important as it is offline, and it contributes to a healthier, more supportive digital environment.

Developing Digital Literacy: Critical Thinking Skills

In an age where misinformation and fake news can spread rapidly, developing strong digital literacy and critical thinking skills is crucial. These skills help your teen navigate the vast amount of information online, distinguishing between credible sources and unreliable content.

- *Evaluating Sources:* Teach your teen how to critically evaluate the sources of the information they encounter online. Encourage them to ask questions like: Who is the author? What is their agenda? Is the information supported by credible evidence? These questions can help them discern between factual content and misinformation. Discuss examples of fake news and how it can spread, emphasizing the importance of verifying information before sharing it.

- *Understanding Algorithms*: Social media platforms use algorithms to determine what content users see. These algorithms are designed to keep users engaged, often by showing content that aligns with their interests and views. Explain to your teen how these algorithms work and how they can create echo chambers—online spaces where one's existing beliefs are constantly reinforced without exposure to differing perspectives. Encourage your teen to seek out diverse viewpoints and be aware of the content they are consuming.

- *Identifying Fake News*: Fake news can be particularly harmful, as it can influence opinions and behaviors based on false information. Teach your teen how to identify fake news by checking for sources, looking at the publication date, and cross-referencing with reputable news outlets. Discuss the dangers of sharing unverified information and the importance of contributing to a well-informed online community.

- *Encouraging Skepticism*: Help your teen develop a healthy skepticism when it comes to online content. Encourage them to question what they see and read, to seek multiple sources before forming an opinion, and to be cautious about believing sensationalized stories or conspiracy theories. Skepticism is a key component of digital literacy, helping your teen become a more informed and discerning user of social media.

Fostering Real-World Connections: Balancing Online and Offline Life

While social media offers valuable opportunities for connection, it's essential that your teen also maintains strong, meaningful relationships in the real world. Balancing their online and offline lives is key to their overall well-being and development.

- *Strengthening Family Bonds*: Make an effort to strengthen family connections by scheduling regular activities that don't involve screens. This could be anything from weekly game nights to cooking together, taking family walks, or simply having device-free meals. These moments help build stronger family bonds and offer a break from the digital world. Encourage open conversations during these times, allowing your teen to share their experiences and concerns.

- *Encouraging Offline Socialization:* Encourage your teen to spend time with friends in person whenever possible. Real-life interactions help develop important social skills and emotional intelligence that cannot be fully cultivated online. Whether it's hanging out at the park, participating in a group activity, or attending social events, these experiences are invaluable. Discuss the importance of face-to-face communication and how it differs from online interactions.

- *Pursuing Hobbies and Interests*: Support your teen in pursuing hobbies and interests that don't involve screens. Whether they're interested in sports, music, art, or something else, these activities provide a healthy balance to their online life and contribute to their personal growth and development. Encourage them to set goals related to their hobbies, such as learning a new skill or participating in a competition, which can boost their confidence and provide a sense of accomplishment.

- *Managing Digital Distractions*: Help your teen manage digital distractions by setting aside specific times for homework, reading, or other focus-intensive activities without interruptions from their devices. Encourage the use of apps that limit distractions, such as those that block social media during study times or track focus periods. Developing the ability to focus and work without digital interruptions is a valuable skill that will benefit your teen in many areas of life.

- *Modeling Balance*: As with many aspects of parenting, your behavior sets the tone. Model a balanced approach to technology use by setting boundaries for yourself, engaging in offline activities, and prioritizing face-to

-face interactions. Your actions can significantly influence how your teen manages their digital habits. Show them that it's possible to enjoy the benefits of technology while still maintaining a healthy and fulfilling offline life.

In this digital age, building healthy habits around social media and technology use is essential for your teen's mental, emotional, and physical well-being. By setting clear boundaries, promoting responsible online behavior, developing critical thinking skills, and encouraging a balance between online and offline activities, you can help your teen pull through the complexities of the digital world with confidence and responsibility.

It is important to remember, the goal is not to eliminate technology from their lives but to integrate it in a way that supports their overall growth and happiness.

Chapter 4:

Privacy and Safety in the Digital Space

In a world where nearly every aspect of life can be shared online, protecting privacy and ensuring safety is more critical than ever. For teens, the allure of social media often comes with a lack of awareness about the potential risks associated with sharing personal information.

This chapter guides you through the essential steps to help your teen understand and manage their digital privacy, safeguard their personal data, and recognize the warning signs of online threats. By fostering a strong foundation in digital safety, you can empower your teen to navigate the online world responsibly and securely.

Understanding and Setting Privacy Controls

Privacy controls are your teen's first line of defense in protecting their online presence. Each social media platform offers a variety of settings that allow users to control who can see their content, who can contact them, and how much personal information is shared. Ensuring that your teen understands and uses these settings is crucial for their safety.

- *Platform-Specific Privacy Settings*: Start by sitting down with your teen and reviewing the privacy settings on each of their social media accounts. Platforms like Instagram, Facebook, TikTok, and Snapchat all have detailed privacy settings that can be customized to limit exposure. Walk through these settings together, explaining what each one does and why it's important. For example, setting an account to private ensures that only approved followers can see their posts, while disabling location services can prevent sharing their whereabouts.

- *Limiting Personal Information*: Encourage your teen to minimize the amount of personal information they share online. This includes details like their full name, home address, phone number, school, and any other information that could be used to identify or locate them. Discuss the potential risks of oversharing, such as identity theft, stalking, or exploitation. Make sure they understand that even seemingly harmless information, like a birthday or pet's name, can be used by malicious actors to guess passwords or answer security questions.

- *Regularly Updating Settings*: Social media platforms frequently update their privacy policies and settings. Encourage your teen to regularly review and update their privacy settings, especially when a platform releases new features or undergoes significant changes. This practice ensures that their accounts remain secure and that they're not unknowingly sharing more than they intend to.

Protecting Personal Information: What Teens Need to Know

The internet is a public space, and once something is posted, it can be challenging—if not impossible—to take it back. Educating your teen about the importance of protecting their personal information is a critical step in keeping them safe online.

- *The Permanence of Online Content*: Help your teen understand that once something is shared online, it can exist indefinitely, even if they delete it later. This is because content can be saved, shared, or archived by others. Discuss examples of how information shared in the past can resurface year's later, potentially impacting future opportunities, such as college admissions or job prospects.

- *Recognizing Phishing and Scams*: Online scams are increasingly sophisticated, and teens are prime targets due to their frequent internet use and relative inexperience. Teach your teen to be cautious of unsolicited messages, emails, or links, especially those asking for personal information or offering something that seems too good to be true. Explain how phishing attempts often mimic legitimate companies or people to trick users into revealing sensitive information. Encourage them to double-check the source before clicking on any links or providing any information.

- *Password Security*: Strong, unique passwords are essential for protecting online accounts. Encourage your teen to create complex passwords that combine letters, numbers, and symbols. Stress the importance of not reusing passwords across different sites and consider using a password manager to keep track of them securely. Additionally, remind them never to share their passwords with anyone, not even close friends, and to change their passwords regularly.

- *Two-Factor Authentication (2FA):* Whenever possible, enable two-factor authentication (2FA) on your teen's accounts. 2FA adds an extra layer of security by requiring a second form of verification—such as a text message code or authentication app—before logging in. This significantly reduces the risk of unauthorized access, even if someone manages to obtain their password.

Safeguarding Against Online Predators and Scams

The anonymity of the internet can make it a breeding ground for predators and scammers who often target teens due to their vulnerability and lack of experience. Teaching your teen how to recognize and respond to these threats is crucial for their safety.

- *Recognizing Red Flags*: Educate your teen about the warning signs of an online predator. These can include someone who asks for personal information early in a conversation, tries to isolate them from their friends or family, or engages in inappropriate or sexual conversations. Make sure they know to never share personal details, meet someone in person that they've only met online, or send photos to anyone they don't know well.

- *Using Reporting and Blocking Features:* Ensure your teen knows how to use the reporting and blocking features available on social media platforms. These tools are designed to help users protect themselves from harassment, bullying, or predatory behavior. Encourage your teen to report any suspicious or inappropriate behavior immediately and to block any users who make them feel uncomfortable.

- *Understanding Common Scams:* Scams targeting teens can take many forms, from fake scholarships and contests to phishing schemes that promise free gifts or discounts. Teach your teen to be skeptical of offers that seem too good to be true and to verify the legitimacy of any offer by checking official websites or contacting companies directly. Additionally, discuss the importance of not sharing financial information online unless it's through a secure and verified channel.

- *Creating a Safe Space for Communication*: Encourage open communication with your teen about their online experiences. Make sure they know they can come to you with any concerns or questions without fear of judgment or punishment. This openness is essential for helping them navigate difficult situations and ensuring they have the support they need to make safe decisions.

Basic Cybersecurity: Keeping Devices and Data Secure

In addition to safeguarding personal information and recognizing online threats, your teen also needs to understand the basics of cybersecurity. Keeping their devices and data secure is essential for protecting against hacking, identity theft, and other cyber threats.

- *Keeping Software Up to Date*: One of the simplest yet most effective ways to protect against cyber threats is by keeping all devices, apps, and software up to date. Updates often include security patches that address vulnerabilities discovered since the last version. Teach your teen the importance of enabling automatic updates on all their devices to ensure they're always protected.

- *Installing and Using Antivirus Software*: Make sure your teen's devices are equipped with up-to-date antivirus software. This software can detect and remove malicious programs like viruses, spyware, and ransomware. Encourage your teen to run regular scans to ensure their devices remain secure and to avoid downloading apps or files from untrusted sources.

- *Practicing Safe Browsing*: Safe browsing habits are essential for avoiding malicious websites and phishing scams. Teach your teen to recognize secure websites by looking for "https://" in the URL and a padlock symbol in the address bar. Encourage them to avoid clicking on suspicious links or pop-ups, and to be cautious when downloading files or software from the internet.

- *Backing Up Data*: Regularly backing up important data—such as photos, schoolwork, and documents—is essential in case of a cyberattack or device failure. Encourage your teen to use cloud services or external hard drives to back up their data. This practice ensures that even if something happens to their device, they won't lose valuable information.

- *Understanding Public Wi-Fi Risks*: Public Wi-Fi networks are convenient but can be insecure, making them prime targets for hackers. Teach your teen to avoid accessing sensitive accounts, such as banking or personal email, while connected to public Wi-Fi. If they must use public Wi-Fi, encourage them to use a virtual private network (VPN) to encrypt their connection and protect their data.

Scouting the digital space with safety and privacy in mind is a critical skill for teens in today's world. By educating your teen on the importance of privacy controls, protecting personal information, recognizing online threats, and practicing basic cybersecurity, you can empower them to manage their online presence responsibly.

These practices not only protect them from immediate risks but also help build a foundation of digital literacy that will serve them throughout their lives.

Chapter 5:

Mental Health and Social Media

Social media has become an integral part of teenagers' lives, offering opportunities for connection, creativity, and self-expression.
However, these platforms can also pose significant risks to mental health, particularly for adolescents who are still developing their sense of self and emotional resilience.

This chapter we explains the complex relationship between social media and mental health, highlighting the potential impacts on your teen's well-being and providing strategies to help them navigate these challenges. By fostering awareness and open communication, you can support your teen in maintaining a healthy relationship with social media.

Recognizing Signs of Social Media-Induced Anxiety and Depression

As social media usage increases, so does the potential for anxiety and depression. The constant exposure to curated images, peer pressure, and online interactions can significantly affect a teen's mental health. Being able to recognize the signs of social media-induced anxiety and depression is crucial for early intervention and support.

- *Changes in Mood and Behavior*: One of the first indicators that social media is negatively impacting your teen's mental health may be noticeable changes in their mood and behavior. These changes can include increased irritability, sadness, or withdrawal from social activities they once enjoyed. If your teen seems particularly down after spending time online, it might be a sign that they are struggling with the content they are engaging with or the interactions they are having.

- *Obsessive Social Media Use:* Pay attention to how much time your teen is spending on social media and whether they seem anxious or agitated when they are not connected. Obsessive checking of social media accounts, even during inappropriate times like meals or late at night, can be a red flag. This behavior often stems from the fear of missing out (FOMO) or the need for constant validation through likes and comments.

- *Sleep Disruption*: The blue light emitted by screens and the mental stimulation from social media can interfere with sleep patterns. If your teen is staying up late to scroll through social media or has trouble falling asleep because they are thinking about online interactions, it could be affecting their overall well-being. Poor sleep can exacerbate symptoms of anxiety and depression, creating a vicious cycle.

- *Social Withdrawal:* While social media is designed to be social, overuse can sometimes lead to social withdrawal in real life. If your teen begins to isolate themselves from family and friends or avoids face-to-face interactions in favor of online communication, it may be time to address their social media habits.

Addressing Body Image and Self-Esteem Challenges

Social media platforms are flooded with images of idealized bodies and lifestyles, often edited or filtered to appear flawless. For teens, who are particularly vulnerable to issues of body image and self-esteem, this can lead to negative self-perception and unhealthy behaviors.

- *Understanding the Impact of Filters and Editing*: It's important to educate your teen about the prevalence of photo editing and filters on social media. Explain that many of the images they see are not realistic representations of everyday life but are instead carefully curated and enhanced. Encourage them to follow accounts that promote body positivity and authenticity rather than those that perpetuate unrealistic standards.

- *Promoting Body Positivity*: Engage in conversations that promote a positive body image, focusing on health, strength, and what their bodies can do, rather than just appearance. Encourage your teen to celebrate their unique qualities and to appreciate diversity in body shapes and sizes. Reinforce the idea that their worth is not determined by how closely they match the images they see online.

- *Encouraging Critical Viewing*: Teach your teen to be a critical viewer of social media content.

Encourage them to question the authenticity of the images they see and to consider the effort that goes into creating a "perfect" post. This critical approach can help them resist the pressure to compare themselves unfavorably to others.

- *Reducing Exposure*: If your teen is struggling with body image issues, it may be helpful to reduce their exposure to certain types of content. Encourage them to unfollow accounts that make them feel bad about themselves and to engage with content that uplifts and empowers them instead.

The Impact of Online Validation and Dopamine Loops

Social media platforms are designed to be engaging, using psychological triggers to keep users coming back. One of the most powerful of these triggers is the dopamine loop, which can lead to a dependency on online validation.

- *Understanding the Dopamine Effect*: When your teen receives a like, comment, or share on social media, their brain releases dopamine, a chemical associated with pleasure and reward. This creates a positive feedback loop, encouraging them to post more and to seek further validation from their peers. Over time, this can lead to a reliance on social media for self-esteem and happiness.

- *The Risks of Validation Seeking:* The pursuit of online validation can be harmful, particularly if your teen begins to equate their self-worth with the number of likes or followers they have. This can lead to a range of negative outcomes, including increased anxiety, depression, and feelings of inadequacy if their posts do not receive the expected level of engagement.

- *Promoting Offline Validation*: Encourage your teen to seek validation through real-life achievements and interactions rather than relying solely on social media. This could include excelling in a hobby, building strong friendships, or achieving personal goals. Remind them that their value is not tied to their online presence but to who they are as a person.

- *Setting Healthy Boundaries*: Help your teen set boundaries around their social media use to reduce the impact of dopamine loops. This might include limiting the time spent on social media, turning off notifications, or taking regular breaks from posting. Encourage them to reflect on how they feel after using social media and to make adjustments if they notice negative patterns.

When to Seek Professional Help: Support Resources

There are times when the effects of social media on your teen's mental health may go beyond what can be managed at home. Knowing when to seek professional help is crucial for their well-being.

- *Identifying When to Seek Help:* If your teen shows persistent signs of anxiety, depression, or other mental health issues that do not improve over time, it may be time to seek professional support. Warning signs include ongoing mood swings, a significant drop in academic performance, withdrawal from social activities, and talk of self-harm or suicide.

- *Exploring Therapy Options:* Various forms of therapy can help teens cope with the mental health challenges posed by social media. Cognitive-behavioral therapy (CBT) is particularly effective, as it helps individuals recognize and change negative thought patterns and behaviors. A therapist can work with your teen to develop healthier ways of interacting with social media and managing their emotions.

- *Utilizing Online Mental Health Resources*: There are numerous online resources available that offer support for teens dealing with mental health issues related to social media. Websites, apps, and online counseling services can provide additional tools and coping strategies. Encourage your teen to explore these resources and consider using them as part of their overall mental health strategy.

- *Creating a Supportive Environment:* Foster an environment at home where your teen feels safe discussing their feelings and experiences with social media. Let them know that it's okay to struggle and that seeking help is a sign of strength, not weakness. Your support can make a significant difference in how they manage the challenges they face.

The relationship between social media and mental health is complex and multifaceted. While social media can offer valuable opportunities for connection and self-expression, it can also pose significant risks to your teen's well-being. By recognizing the signs of social media-induced anxiety and depression, addressing body image and self-esteem challenges, understanding the impact of online validation, and knowing when to seek professional help, you can help your teen go through these challenges more effectively.

Chapter 6:

Effective Communication with Your Teen

In the digital age, maintaining open and honest communication with your teen is more important than ever. As they navigate the complexities of social media, peer pressure, and the challenges of adolescence, your role as a supportive and understanding parent is crucial.

In chapter 6 we provide strategies for fostering effective communication with your teen, helping you build a strong relationship based on trust, mutual respect, and understanding. By mastering these communication techniques, you can create an environment where your teen feels safe discussing their online experiences and seeking your guidance.

Initiating Conversations: How to Talk About Social Media

Starting a conversation about social media use can be tricky, especially if your teen feels that their privacy is being invaded or that they are being judged. However, these discussions are essential for helping them navigate the digital world safely and responsibly.

- *Choose the Right Time and Place*: Timing is everything when it comes to initiating conversations with your teen. Choose a moment when both you and your teen are relaxed and free from distractions. This could be during a car ride, a walk, or a quiet moment at home. Avoid bringing up the topic during a disagreement or when emotions are running high.

- *Use Open-Ended Questions*: Encourage your teen to share their thoughts and experiences by asking open-ended questions. Instead of asking, "Did you spend too much time on your phone today?" try, "What's the most interesting thing you saw online today?" This approach invites them to talk more freely and gives you insight into their online activities without making them feel defensive.

- *Show Genuine Interest:* When discussing social media, it's important to show that you are genuinely interested in their world. Ask them to explain the platforms they use, the content they enjoy, and why they like certain apps or influencers. This not only helps you understand their online behavior but also shows that you respect their interests.

- *Avoid Judgment:* Teens are more likely to open up if they feel they won't be judged. Approach conversations about social media with curiosity rather than criticism. If your teen feels they are being attacked or judged, they may shut down or become defensive. Instead, focus on understanding their perspective and offering guidance rather than issuing directives.

- *Relate to Their Experiences:* Share your own experiences with technology and social interactions, even if they are from a different era. Let your teen know that while the platforms may be different, the core challenges—like fitting in, dealing with peer pressure, and finding your identity—are timeless. This can help bridge the generational gap and make your teen feel understood.

Active Listening: Understanding Your Teen's Perspective

Listening is one of the most powerful tools in effective communication. When your teen feels heard and understood, they are more likely to share their thoughts and concerns with you, creating a foundation of trust.

- *Practice Reflective Listening*: Reflective listening involves paraphrasing what your teen has said to show that you are paying attention and understanding their point of view. For example, if your teen says, "I hate how everyone on Instagram seems perfect," you might respond, "It sounds like you're feeling frustrated by the unrealistic standards you see online." This technique helps validate their feelings and encourages them to keep talking.

- *Avoid Interrupting:* Let your teen finish their thoughts before you respond. Interrupting can make them feel like their opinions are not valued or that you are more interested in giving advice than hearing what they have to say. Give them the space to express themselves fully before you offer your input.

- *Use Nonverbal Cues*: Nonverbal communication, such as nodding, maintaining eye contact, and using open body language, can reinforce that you are listening and engaged. These cues show that you are fully present in the conversation and care about what they have to say.

- *Acknowledge Their Emotions:* Teens often experience intense emotions, and it's important to acknowledge these feelings without dismissing them. If your teen is upset about something they saw online, validate their emotions by saying something like, "I can see why that would make you feel angry" or "Understandably, you're feeling sad about this." This approach helps them feel supported and understood.

- *Encourage Them to Express Themselves*: Let your teen know that it's okay to share their feelings, even if they are negative or difficult to express. Create an environment where they feel safe to talk about their fears, frustrations, and concerns without fear of repercussions. This openness is crucial for building trust and maintaining a strong relationship.

Conflict Resolution: Handling Disagreements Constructively

Disagreements are inevitable, especially when it comes to setting boundaries around social media use or addressing online behavior. How you handle these conflicts can either strengthen or weaken your relationship with your teen.

- *Stay Calm and Composed:* When a disagreement arises, it's important to remain calm and avoid raising your voice or becoming confrontational. A heated response can escalate the situation and lead to a power struggle. Instead, take a deep breath and approach the conversation with a cool head.

- *Focus on the Issue, Not the Person*: Address the behavior or issue at hand without attacking your teen's character. For example, instead of saying, "You're always glued to your phone," try, "I've noticed that you've been spending a lot of time on your phone lately, and I'm concerned about how it might be affecting your sleep." This approach separates the person from the behavior, making it easier to discuss solutions.

- *Seek Compromise*: Look for ways to compromise when setting rules or resolving conflicts. For instance, if your teen wants to stay up late on weekends to use social media, you might agree to extend their bedtime slightly while also setting limits on screen time before bed. Compromise shows that you respect their autonomy while still upholding your concerns.

- Use "I" Statements: When discussing issues, use "I" statements to express your feelings without placing blame. For example, say, "I feel worried when you spend so much time online because I'm concerned about your well-being," rather than, "You're always online, and it's unhealthy." This language fosters a more constructive dialogue and reduces defensiveness.

- *Encourage Problem-Solving*: Empower your teen to be part of the solution by asking for their input on how to address the issue. For example, if they're struggling to manage their screen time, ask, "What do you think would help you stay on track with your goals?" This collaborative approach encourages responsibility and helps them develop problem-solving skills.

Building Trust: Creating Open Dialogue About Online Activities

Trust is the cornerstone of any healthy parent-teen relationship. Building and maintaining trust involves transparency, honesty, and mutual respect. When your teen trusts you, they are more likely to come to you with their online experiences, whether positive or negative.

- *Be Transparent About Your Concerns:* Explain to your teen why you're concerned about certain aspects of their online behavior without making them feel like they're being spied on. For example, you might say, "I know social media is important to you, but I worry about some of the risks, like cyberbullying or oversharing. Let's talk about how we can make sure you're safe online." This transparency helps your teen understand that your intentions are protective, not punitive.

- *Respect Their Privacy:* While it's important to be aware of what your teen is doing online, respecting their privacy is equally crucial. Avoid snooping or demanding access to all their accounts unless there's a clear and urgent reason to do so. Instead, foster an environment where they feel comfortable sharing their online experiences with you voluntarily.

- *Encourage Open Communication:* Let your teen know that they can come to you with any concerns or questions about their online experiences without fear of punishment. If they make a mistake or encounter something troubling online, assure them that you will listen and help them navigate the situation rather than immediately resorting to discipline.

- *Model Trustworthy Behavior*: Trust is a two-way street. Model the behavior you expect from your teen by being honest, reliable, and consistent in your actions. If you say you're going to do something—like respecting their privacy—make sure you follow through. Your actions will demonstrate that you can be trusted, encouraging your teen to be trustworthy in return.

- *Celebrate Their Online Achievements*: Acknowledge and celebrate the positive aspects of your teen's online life. Whether they've created something they're proud of, learned a new skill, or formed a healthy online community, recognizing these achievements helps reinforce the idea that you're supportive of their digital life, not just critical.

Effective communication with your teen is essential in helping them navigate the complexities of social media and the digital world. By initiating open conversations, practicing active listening, handling conflicts constructively, and building trust, you can create a strong foundation for your relationship.

This foundation will not only help your teen feel supported and understood but also empower them to make informed, responsible decisions in their online and offline lives.

Chapter 7:

Fostering Positive Digital Citizenship

In a world where much of our social interaction occurs online, fostering positive digital citizenship is crucial. For teens, understanding how to explore the digital world with respect, responsibility, and integrity is essential for their personal development and the well-being of the online communities they engage with.

This book would help guide your teen in becoming a responsible digital citizen, focusing on empathy, authenticity, and the positive impact they can make through their online presence.

Teaching Empathy and Respect in Online Interactions

Empathy and respect are foundational elements of positive digital citizenship. In an environment where anonymity can sometimes lead to harsh or thoughtless behavior, teaching your teen to approach online interactions with empathy is more important than ever.

- *Understanding the Impact of Words*: Start by helping your teen understand that words have power, even online. Just as in face-to-face interactions, what they say or type can have a lasting impact on others. Discuss the importance of thinking before posting, considering how their words might be received, and the potential consequences of hurtful or insensitive comments.

- *Promoting Kindness and Support*: Encourage your teen to use their online presence to spread positivity.

This can include offering words of encouragement, supporting friends or peers in need, and standing up against cyberbullying. By promoting kindness, your teen can contribute to a more supportive and inclusive online community.

- *Practicing Empathy in Online Disagreements:* Disagreements are inevitable, both online and offline. Teach your teen how to navigate conflicts with empathy and respect. This involves listening to others' perspectives, responding thoughtfully rather than reactively, and avoiding personal attacks. Encourage them to take a step back if a conversation becomes heated and to consider the other person's feelings before responding.

- *Avoiding the Spread of Negativity*: The internet can be a breeding ground for negativity, with gossip, rumors, and mean-spirited content often going viral. Talk to your teen about the importance of not participating in or spreading harmful content.

Instead, encourage them to be a voice of reason and to report harmful behavior when they see it.

Encouraging Authenticity: Being True to Oneself Online

In a digital landscape dominated by filters, curated images, and the pressure to present a perfect life, authenticity can be a breath of fresh air. Encouraging your teen to be authentic online can help them build self-confidence and foster genuine connections.

- *Understanding the Pressure to Conform*: Many teens feel pressured to conform to certain online trends or to present an idealized version of themselves to gain likes, followers, or acceptance. Discuss this pressure with your teen and help them understand that they don't need to fit a mold to be valued or respected online.

- *Celebrating Individuality*: Encourage your teen to express their true self online, sharing their interests, opinions, and creativity in ways that reflect who they are. Whether it's posting about a hobby they love, sharing their thoughts on a topic they care about, or simply being honest in their interactions, authenticity can help them stand out positively.

- *Balancing Privacy and Authenticity:* While it's important to be authentic, it's also essential to balance this with privacy. Teach your teen to think carefully about what they share online, ensuring that they are comfortable with the information being public and that it doesn't compromise their safety or privacy. Authenticity doesn't mean sharing everything; it means being genuine in what they choose to share.

- *Avoiding the Comparison Trap*: Remind your teen that what they see online is often a highlight reel, not an accurate representation of someone's entire life.

Encourage them to avoid comparing themselves to others and to focus on their own journey. Authenticity means embracing who they are, not trying to be someone else.

Using Social Media for Good: Promoting Positive Causes

Social media can be a powerful tool for change when used for good. Many teens are passionate about social justice, environmental issues, and other causes that matter to them. Encouraging your teen to use their online presence to promote positive causes can help them feel empowered and make a real difference in the world.

- *Finding and Supporting Causes*: Help your teen identify causes they are passionate about and explore ways to support them online. This could involve sharing informative content, participating in online campaigns, or raising awareness through their own posts. Discuss the importance of researching causes thoroughly to ensure they are legitimate and align with their values.

- *Engaging in Digital Activism:* Digital activism involves using social media to advocate for change. Whether it's signing petitions, joining virtual events, or engaging in discussions about important issues, digital activism allows teens to use their voice for good. Encourage your teen to get involved in causes they care about while being mindful of the impact their words and actions can have.

- *Connecting with Like-Minded Communities*: Social media offers opportunities to connect with others who share similar passions and goals. Encourage your teen to join online communities or groups focused on positive causes. These connections can provide support, inspiration, and a sense of belonging, reinforcing the idea that they are not alone in their efforts.

- *Creating Positive Content:* If your teen enjoys creating content, encourage them to use their skills to promote positivity and awareness. Whether it's making videos, writing blog posts, or designing graphics, they can contribute to important conversations and inspire others to get involved. Highlight the importance of ensuring that their content is respectful, accurate, and aligns with the positive message they want to share.

Leading by Example: How Your Social Media Habits Influence Your Teen

As a parent, your social media habits have a significant impact on your teen. Modeling positive behavior online can influence how they approach their digital presence and interactions.

- *Demonstrating Respectful Online Behavior:* Your teen is likely to mirror how you interact online, so it's important to model respectful behavior. This includes being polite in comments, avoiding online arguments, and showing empathy in your interactions. If you encounter a disagreement, handle it maturely, showing your teen how to navigate conflicts without resorting to negativity.

- *Balancing Online and Offline Life:* Show your teen the importance of balancing screen time with offline activities. Make a conscious effort to put away devices during family time, meals, and other important moments. By prioritizing real-world connections, you demonstrate that while social media is a tool for communication, it should not replace face-to-face interactions.

- *Being Mindful of Privacy:* Model good practices around privacy by being selective about what you share online. Discuss with your teen why you choose to keep certain aspects of your life private and how you ensure that your personal information is protected. This sets a standard for them to follow in managing their online privacy.

- *Promoting Positivity:* Use your social media platforms to spread positivity and support others. Whether it's sharing uplifting stories, celebrating others' successes, or engaging in constructive discussions, your actions set an example of how to use social media for good. Encourage your teen to do the same by being a positive force in their online communities.

Fostering positive digital citizenship in your teen is about more than just teaching them how to behave online; it's about helping them understand the broader impact they can have on the digital world. By teaching empathy, encouraging authenticity, promoting the use of social media for good, and leading by example, you can guide your teen toward becoming a responsible and impactful digital citizen.

Chapter 8:

Managing Social Media Through Life Transitions

Life transitions, such as starting high school, moving to a new city, or even going through a breakup, can significantly impact how teens use social media. During these times, social media can either serve as a source of support or exacerbate stress and anxiety.

This chapter teaches how to help your teen manage their social media use during significant life changes, ensuring it remains a positive tool rather than a source of added pressure. By providing guidance and understanding, you can help your teen go through these transitions more smoothly.

Balancing Academics and Social Media: Strategies for Success

As your teen progresses through their academic journey, the demands of schoolwork, extracurricular activities, and social life increase. Balancing these responsibilities with social media use can be challenging but essential for their success and well-being.

- *Establishing Priorities:* Help your teen prioritize their responsibilities by discussing the importance of balancing academics with social media. Emphasize that while staying connected with friends is important, it should not come at the expense of their education. Encourage them to set clear priorities, such as completing homework before engaging in social media or setting aside specific times for study and online interaction.

- *Creating a Study Schedule*: Work with your teen to develop a study schedule that incorporates time for social media in a way that doesn't interfere with their academic goals. This might involve designating specific blocks of time for social media use, such as after school or during a break from studying. By including social media in their schedule, your teen can enjoy it without it becoming a distraction from their studies.

- *Using Technology to Stay Organized*: Encourage your teen to use technology to their advantage by utilizing apps and tools that help them stay organized. Calendar apps, task managers, and even study-focused apps like Forest can help them manage their time effectively while minimizing distractions. These tools can provide a structured approach to balancing academics and social media.

- *Encouraging Breaks and Offline Time*: Promote the importance of taking regular breaks from both studying and social media to prevent burnout. Encourage your teen to engage in offline activities that help them relax and recharge, such as exercise, hobbies, or spending time with family. These breaks can improve their focus and overall well-being.

- *Monitoring Academic Performance*: Keep an eye on your teen's academic performance to ensure that social media is not negatively impacting their grades. If you notice a decline in their schoolwork or an increase in late assignments, it may be time to reassess their social media habits and make necessary adjustments.

Exploring Social Changes: Friendships and Relationships

Social transitions, such as making new friends, starting or ending a relationship, or changing schools, can significantly influence how teens use social media. These periods of change can be emotionally charged, and social media can either support or hinder their adjustment.

- *Supporting New Friendships:* When your teen is forming new friendships, social media can be a valuable tool for staying connected and getting to know others better. Encourage them to use social media positively by joining group chats, following new friends, and participating in online communities related to their interests. However, remind them to also invest in face-to-face interactions, as these are crucial for building deeper, more meaningful relationships.

- *Handling Breakups Online*: Breakups can be particularly challenging for teens, especially when they play out on social media. Help your teen navigate this difficult time by discussing the pros and cons of staying connected with an ex online. Encourage them to consider unfollowing or muting their ex to avoid constant reminders and the temptation to compare themselves to their ex's new relationships. Additionally, remind them to avoid posting hurtful or passive-aggressive content that could escalate the situation.

- *Managing Online Drama*: Social changes can sometimes lead to online drama, such as gossip, rumors, or conflicts. Teach your teen strategies for managing and avoiding online drama, such as not engaging in arguments, reporting or blocking problematic users, and seeking out positive interactions instead. Encourage them to talk to you or another trusted adult if they are feeling overwhelmed by online drama.

- *Supporting Friendships During Moves*: If your teen is moving to a new city or school, social media can be a lifeline for maintaining old friendships while forming new ones. Encourage your teen to use social media to stay in touch with friends they're leaving behind while also exploring new social circles online. This balance can help them feel more secure during the transition.

Supporting Teens Through Online Challenges: Breakups, Rumors, and More

The online world can amplify the emotional challenges that come with life transitions, such as breakups, rumors, or conflicts with friends. It's important to provide your teen with the tools and support they need to navigate these challenges effectively.

- *Coping with Breakups*: Social media can make breakups more difficult by keeping reminders of the relationship constantly visible. Encourage your teen to take a break from social media if they find it too painful to see their ex's posts. If they choose to stay online, suggest that they focus on content that uplifts them and reminds them of their own strengths and interests. This could be a good time for them to explore new hobbies or interests that they can share on social media, helping them move forward positively.

- *Dealing with Online Rumors*: Rumors can spread quickly on social media, and the impact can be devastating for teens. If your teen is the subject of online rumors, offer your support by listening to their concerns and helping them develop a plan to address the situation. This might involve confronting the rumor privately with those involved, reporting harmful content, or seeking help from school authorities if the situation escalates. Remind your teen that rumors often say more about the person spreading them than about the person targeted.

- *Handling Cyberbullying:* Cyberbullying can be particularly intense during life transitions, as teens may feel more vulnerable or isolated. Encourage your teen to talk to you about any bullying they experience online, and work together to address it. This might involve blocking the bully, reporting the behavior to the platform, or even involving school officials or law enforcement if the situation is serious. Emphasize that they should not suffer in silence and that help is available.

- *Rebuilding Confidence:* Life transitions and online challenges can take a toll on your teen's self-esteem. Encourage them to engage in activities that help rebuild their confidence, whether it's spending time with supportive friends, pursuing a passion, or setting new personal goals. Social media can be a place to celebrate these achievements and find encouragement from others who share similar experiences.

Preparing for the Future: Social Media and College Admissions

As your teen approaches the end of high school, social media can play a role in their future opportunities, including college admissions. It's important to help them understand how their online presence can impact their future and how to use social media responsibly during this critical time.

- *Understanding the Impact of Social Media on College Admissions*: Many colleges and universities now consider applicants' social media presence as part of the admissions process. Admissions officers may look at social media profiles to gain insight into an applicant's character, interests, and fit for the school. Discuss with your teen the importance of maintaining a positive online presence that reflects their values and goals.

- *Curating a Positive Online Image*: Encourage your teen to review their social media profiles and remove any content that could be viewed negatively by college admissions officers. This includes posts that are inappropriate, controversial, or that could be misinterpreted. Suggest that they focus on sharing content that highlights their achievements, interests, and positive contributions to their community.

- *Using Social Media to Enhance Applications:* Social media can also be used to enhance college applications by showcasing talents, extracurricular activities, and leadership roles. For example, a teen who is passionate about art might use Instagram to display their portfolio, while a student involved in community service might share their volunteer experiences on Facebook or LinkedIn. These platforms can serve as a supplement to traditional application materials, offering a more comprehensive view of who they are.

- *Networking for the Future*: Encourage your teen to use platforms like LinkedIn to start building a professional network early on. This can involve connecting with teachers, mentors, or professionals in fields they are interested in. Networking can provide valuable opportunities for internships, scholarships, and future career prospects.

- Being Mindful of Privacy Settings: Remind your teen to review and update their privacy settings on all social media platforms, especially as they approach the college application process. This ensures that they have control over what admissions officers and others can see. Encourage them to think carefully about what they post and to always assume that anything shared online could be viewed by a broader audience.

Life transitions are often challenging for teens, and social media can either help them go through these changes or add to the stress. By providing guidance on balancing academics with social media, supporting them through social changes, helping them handle online challenges, and preparing them for the future, you can ensure that social media remains a positive and supportive tool during these times.

Chapter 9:

Parenting Strategies for the Digital Future

As technology continues to evolve at a rapid pace, the challenges and opportunities it presents are constantly changing. To effectively guide your teen through the digital landscape, it's essential to stay informed about emerging trends, equip them with the skills needed for a digital career, and foster lifelong digital literacy.

Strategies for parenting in a digital future, helping you prepare your teen for the world they will soon navigate independently. By adopting these strategies, you can ensure that your teen is not only safe online but also well-prepared to thrive in a digital world.

Staying Ahead: Emerging Social Media Trends

The digital world is ever-evolving, with new platforms, features, and trends emerging regularly. Staying ahead of these changes is crucial for understanding the environment your teen is engaging with and guiding them through it safely.

- *Keeping Up with New Platforms*: New social media platforms frequently appear on the scene, each offering unique features that attract teens. As a parent, it's important to stay informed about these emerging platforms. This doesn't mean you need to become an expert, but having a basic understanding of what these platforms offer and how they are used can help you better communicate with your teen about their online activities. Consider setting aside time each month to research the latest trends or ask your teen to explain the newest apps they are using.

- *Understanding the Appeal of New Features*: Even on established platforms, new features and updates can change how your teen interacts online. Whether it's the introduction of new algorithms, changes to privacy settings, or the addition of new content formats (like Instagram Reels or TikTok's extended video lengths), understanding these changes can help you stay connected to your teen's digital world. Encourage your teen to discuss these updates with you, so you can both stay informed.

- *Recognizing the Risks and Benefits:* Every new platform or feature comes with its own set of risks and benefits. As your teen explores these digital spaces, guide them in evaluating the potential impacts on their privacy, mental health, and overall well-being. Discuss the importance of being cautious when adopting new technologies and the value of taking time to understand them before diving in.

- *Encouraging a Balanced Approach:* While it's natural for teens to be excited about the latest digital trends, encourage them to take a balanced approach. Remind them that not every trend or platform will be beneficial, and it's okay to opt out of participating if it doesn't align with their values or needs. Fostering critical thinking about digital trends helps them make informed decisions and avoid potential pitfalls.

Preparing Teens for a Digital Career: Skills and Opportunities

As the job market increasingly shifts towards digital and tech-based roles, equipping your teen with the skills needed for a digital career can open up a world of opportunities. Whether they aspire to work in technology, digital marketing, content creation, or any number of other fields, developing digital skills is essential.

- *Exploring Digital Career Paths*: Help your teen explore potential digital career paths by discussing their interests and strengths. Whether they're interested in coding, graphic design, video production, or social media management, there are numerous avenues to explore. Encourage them to research different careers, talk to professionals in the field, and consider what skills they might need to develop.

- *Developing Essential Digital Skills:* In today's job market, digital literacy is a fundamental requirement. Encourage your teen to develop essential digital skills such as coding, digital marketing, graphic design, and content creation. There are numerous online resources, courses, and tutorials available that can help them build these skills. Platforms like Codecademy, Coursera, and

Khan Academy offer courses that cater to various skill levels and interests.

- *Building a Digital Portfolio:* Encourage your teen to start building a digital portfolio that showcases their skills and projects. Whether it's a personal website, a blog, or a collection of digital art, a portfolio can be a valuable tool when applying for internships, scholarships, or jobs. Help them understand the importance of presenting their work professionally and keeping their portfolio updated.

- *Networking in the Digital World*: Networking is a crucial part of building a career, and the digital world offers numerous opportunities to connect with professionals and mentors. Encourage your teen to create a LinkedIn profile and start building their professional network early. They can join groups related to their interests, participate in online forums, and connect with industry professionals who can offer guidance and support.

- *Understanding the Importance of a Positive Online Presence*: As your teen prepares for a digital career, remind them that their online presence can impact their professional opportunities. Encourage them to curate their social media profiles to reflect their goals and values. This includes being mindful of what they post, how they engage with others, and the image they project online. A positive online presence can set them apart in a competitive job market.

Lifelong Digital Literacy: Cultivating Future Skills

Digital literacy is not just about understanding how to use technology; it's about developing the skills needed to adapt to an ever-changing digital landscape. As new technologies emerge, your teen will need to continually update their knowledge and skills to stay relevant.

- *Fostering a Growth Mindset:* Encourage your teen to adopt a growth mindset when it comes to digital literacy. This means being open to learning new skills, embracing challenges, and understanding that mastery takes time and effort. A growth mindset helps them stay adaptable and resilient in the face of technological change.

- *Encouraging Continuous Learning:* The digital world is constantly evolving, and continuous learning is key to staying ahead. Encourage your teen to seek out new learning opportunities, whether it's through online courses, workshops, or self-directed study. Help them develop the habit of regularly updating their skills and staying informed about industry trends.

- *Promoting Critical Thinking and Problem-Solving*: Critical thinking and problem-solving are essential skills in the digital age. Encourage your teen to question the information they encounter online, analyze data, and approach problems methodically. These skills are valuable not only in digital careers but in navigating the broader world of information and technology.

- *Staying Informed About Emerging Technologies*: Help your teen stay informed about emerging technologies that could impact their future, such as artificial intelligence, blockchain, or virtual reality. Discuss the potential applications and implications of these technologies, and explore how they might influence various industries. This awareness can help them identify opportunities and prepare for future challenges.

- *Building Digital Ethics and Responsibility*: Digital literacy also involves understanding the ethical implications of technology. Teach your teen about the importance of digital ethics, including issues like data privacy, cybersecurity, and the responsible use of technology. Encourage them to think about how their actions online affect others and to use technology in ways that are ethical and responsible.

Adapting to Technological Changes: Continuous Learning

As technology continues to advance, the ability to adapt and learn new skills is increasingly important. Preparing your teen for this reality involves fostering a mindset of lifelong learning and helping them develop the tools they need to stay relevant in a rapidly changing world.

- *Adapting to New Tools and Platforms*: Encourage your teen to stay curious about new tools, platforms, and technologies. Whether it's learning how to use new software, exploring the potential of a new social media platform, or experimenting with emerging technologies, adaptability is key. Teach them to approach new technologies with an open mind and a willingness to learn.

- *Encouraging Experimentation and Innovation:* The digital world offers endless opportunities for experimentation and innovation. Encourage your teen to try new things, whether it's coding a simple app, starting a blog, or creating digital art. This spirit of experimentation can lead to the discovery of new passions and the development of valuable skills.

- *Preparing for Future Career Shifts:* The digital age has brought about significant changes in the job market, with many careers evolving or disappearing due to automation and technological advancements. Help your teen understand the importance of staying adaptable and being prepared for potential career shifts. This might involve developing a diverse skill set, staying informed about industry trends, and being open to exploring new career paths.

- *Emphasizing the Importance of Soft Skills*: While technical skills are important, soft skills like communication, collaboration, and emotional intelligence are equally valuable in the digital age. Encourage your teen to develop these skills alongside their digital literacy. Effective communication, teamwork, and the ability to navigate complex social interactions are crucial for success in any career.

- *Staying Connected to the Real World*: Finally, remind your teen of the importance of staying connected to the real world, even as they embrace digital technology. Please encourage them to engage in face-to-face interactions, build strong relationships, and participate in activities that don't involve screens. This balance between the digital and real worlds is essential for overall well-being and personal growth.

Preparing your teen for the digital future involves more than just teaching them how to use technology;

it's about equipping them with the skills, mindset, and ethics needed to go through a rapidly changing world. By staying informed about emerging trends, helping them develop digital literacy, and fostering a continuous learning mindset, you can ensure they are ready to thrive in whatever the future holds.

Chapter 10:

Tools, Resources, and Support for Parents

As the digital landscape continues to evolve, it's essential for parents to have access to the right tools, resources, and support systems to guide their teens effectively. This chapter provides a comprehensive overview of the tools available to help monitor and manage social media use, educational resources to deepen your understanding, and support systems to ensure both you and your teen are well-equipped to navigate the digital world.

📱 Apps and Tools for Monitoring and Managing Social Media Use

Monitoring and managing your teen's social media use is a crucial aspect of digital parenting. Fortunately, there are a variety of apps and tools available that can help you keep track of your teen's online activities and ensure they are using social media responsibly.

- *Parental Control Apps*: Parental control apps like "Qustodio", "Net Nanny", and "Bark" offer comprehensive monitoring solutions that allow you to track your teen's online activity, set screen time limits, and block inappropriate content. These apps can provide you with detailed reports on your teen's usage patterns, helping you identify any potential issues early on. Many of these apps also offer features like location tracking and alerts for concerning content, giving you peace of mind.

- *Screen Time Management:* Apps like **Screen Time** (built into iOS devices) and **Google Family Link** (for Android devices) allow you to set limits on the amount of time your teen spends on their devices. These tools can help you create a balanced schedule that encourages healthy screen time habits while ensuring your teen has ample time for other activities.

- *Social Media Monitoring:* Tools like 'Bark' and 'MMGuardian' are specifically designed to monitor social media activity, alerting you to potential risks such as cyberbullying, online predators, or inappropriate content. These apps can monitor platforms like Instagram, Snapchat, and TikTok, giving you insight into what your teen is encountering online.

- *Website and Content Filtering*: If you're concerned about the content your teen might be exposed to online, consider using content filtering tools like **OpenDNS** or **Kaspersky Safe Kids**. These tools allow you to block specific websites, categories of content, or even search results that you deem inappropriate or harmful. This can help create a safer online environment for your teen.

- *Communication and Agreement Tools*: Creating a family media agreement can be an effective way to set expectations around social media use. Tools like 'Common Sense Media's Family Media Agreement' provide templates that you can customize to fit your family's needs. These agreements can cover everything from screen time limits to rules about online behavior, helping to ensure everyone is on the same page.

Recommended Reading: Websites, and Organizations

Continuing to educate yourself about the digital world is key to being an informed and effective digital parent. Here are some recommended resources that can help you deepen your understanding and stay updated on the latest trends and challenges.

- **Websites:**

- *Common Sense Media*: A comprehensive resource for parents, Common Sense Media offers reviews of apps, games, and movies, as well as articles and advice on managing technology use in families.

- *ConnectSafely*: This nonprofit organization provides a wealth of resources on online safety, including guides for parents on how to talk to their kids about internet safety, privacy, and social media use.

- *Cyberbullying Research Center*: Dedicated to understanding and preventing cyberbullying, this website offers research, resources, and tips for parents, educators, and teens.

- **Organizations:**

- *Family Online Safety Institute (FOSI):* FOSI works to make the online world safer for families by providing research, resources, and best practices for digital parenting.

- *The Internet Keep Safe Coalition (iKeepSafe):* iKeepSafe offers tools and resources to help parents, educators, and policymakers protect children's privacy and safety online.

- *StopBullying.gov:* This government website provides information and resources to prevent and address bullying, including cyberbullying, with specific guidance for parents and educators.

👣 Sample Family Media Agreements: Setting Clear Expectations

Creating a family media agreement is an excellent way to set clear expectations around social media and screen time. A well-crafted agreement can help prevent conflicts and ensure that everyone in the family understands the rules and boundaries.

- *Creating a Custom Agreement*: Begin by discussing the importance of a family media agreement with your teen. Explain that the goal is to create a balanced approach to technology use that benefits everyone. Work together to establish rules that everyone agrees on, such as screen time limits, appropriate online behavior, and consequences for breaking the rules.

- Topics to Include:

- *Screen Time Limits*: Set clear limits on how much time your teen can spend on social media each day or week. You might also include rules about when and where screens can be used (e.g., no phones at the dinner table or after bedtime).

- Online Behavior: Outline expectations for online behavior, including how to interact with others, what to post, and how to handle negative situations like cyberbullying. Emphasize the importance of respect, empathy, and honesty in all online interactions.

- Privacy and Security: Include guidelines on protecting personal information, using privacy settings, and avoiding sharing too much online. Discuss the importance of keeping passwords secure and not sharing them with others.

- Consequences: Clearly define the consequences for breaking the rules outlined in the agreement. Make sure the consequences are fair and consistent, and that your teen understands them before signing the agreement.

- Reviewing and Updating the Agreement: As your teen grows and technology evolves, it's important to revisit and update your family media agreement. Set a regular time, such as the beginning of each school

year, to review the agreement and make any necessary changes.

🆘 Mental Health and Support Resources: Where to Get Help

If you or your teen are struggling with the challenges of digital life, it's important to know where to turn for help. There are numerous resources available to support both mental health and online safety.

- Mental Health Support:
- National Suicide Prevention Lifeline: Available 24/7, this provides confidential support for anyone in distress, including teens who may be struggling with the pressures of social media.

 - *Crisis Text Line:* A free, confidential service that provides support for people in crisis. Teens can text the service to connect with a trained counselor who can help them navigate their challenges.

- *Therapy and Counseling Services*: If your teen is experiencing significant mental health issues related to social media, consider seeking the help of a licensed therapist or counselor. Cognitive-behavioral therapy (CBT) is particularly effective in addressing anxiety, depression, and other issues related to digital life.

- **Online Safety Support:**

 - *CyberTipline*: Operated by the National Center for Missing & Exploited Children, the CyberTipline allows you to report incidents of online exploitation, such as child pornography or online enticement.

- *National Bullying Prevention Center*: This organization provides resources and support for those dealing with bullying, including cyberbullying. They offer tools for parents, teens, and educators to help prevent and address bullying.

- *NetSmartz*: A program of the National Center for Missing & Exploited Children, NetSmartz offers resources for parents and teens on how to stay safe online, including educational videos, activities, and guides.

By leveraging the right tools, resources, and support systems, you can effectively guide your teen through the challenges of the digital age. Monitoring apps, educational resources, and mental health support are all valuable assets in your digital parenting toolkit.

With these resources at your disposal, you can create a safe, supportive environment that empowers your teen to navigate social media and the internet with confidence and responsibility.

.

🎯 Conclusion:

Empowering Parents and Teens in the Digital World

Exploring the digital world as a parent is no small feat. The rapid evolution of technology and the ever-changing landscape of social media present both challenges and opportunities for today's teens. Throughout this book, we've explored various aspects of digital life—from the psychological impacts of social media to fostering positive digital citizenship, managing online safety, and preparing for the digital future.

As we conclude, it's important to remember that the goal of digital parenting isn't just to protect your teen from the potential harms of technology but to empower them to use it responsibly, creatively, and effectively. By building strong communication, setting clear boundaries, and staying informed about the latest trends and tools, you can help your teen develop a healthy relationship with technology that will serve them well throughout their lives.

↻ Recap: Supporting Healthy Digital Habits and Strong Relationships

Throughout this book, we've covered a broad range of topics designed to help you support your teen in their digital journey. Here's a brief recap of the key strategies discussed:

- **Building Healthy Digital Habits**: Encourage balanced screen time, promote responsible online behavior, and help your teen develop critical thinking skills to navigate the vast amount of information they encounter online. By setting clear boundaries and fostering open communication, you can help your teen maintain a healthy relationship with social media.

- **Promoting Positive Digital Citizenship**: Teach your teen the importance of empathy, respect, and authenticity in their online interactions. Encourage them to use social media for good by supporting causes they care about and being a positive influence in their digital communities. Lead by example, demonstrating respectful and responsible online behavior.

- **Managing Life Transitions:** Support your teen through major life changes, such as starting a new school, navigating friendships, or handling breakups, by guiding how to use social media as a tool for connection and support, rather than a source of stress. Help them prepare for the future by curating a positive online presence and developing the skills needed for digital careers.

- **Preparing for the Digital Future**: Equip your teen with the skills and mindset needed to thrive in an ever-evolving digital world. Encourage continuous learning, foster a growth mindset, and emphasize the importance of digital literacy and ethics. Help them explore potential digital career paths and build a strong professional network.

- **Utilizing Tools and Resources**: Leverage apps, parental control tools, and educational resources to monitor and manage your teen's social media use effectively. Create a family media agreement to set clear expectations, and seek out support systems when needed, whether for mental health or online safety.

❣ Encouraging Growth and Independence in the Digital Age

As your teen grows, so too will their independence in navigating the digital world. Your role as a parent is to provide the foundation they need to make informed, responsible decisions on their own. Encourage them to take ownership of their digital habits, learn from their experiences, and seek out opportunities to grow.

- *Fostering Self-Responsibility:* As your teen matures, gradually shift the responsibility of managing their online presence and screen time to them. This involves trusting them to make good choices, while still being available for guidance and support when needed. Empower them to recognize the impact of their actions online and to take steps to correct any mistakes.

- *Encouraging Exploration and Creativity:* The digital world offers endless opportunities for exploration and creativity. Encourage your teen to pursue their interests, try new things, and express themselves in ways that are meaningful to them. Whether it's through digital art, content creation, coding, or online activism, support their efforts to make a positive impact.

- *Promoting Lifelong Learning:* Emphasize the importance of continuous learning in the digital age. Encourage your teen to stay curious, seek out new skills, and adapt to technological changes. This mindset will not only help them succeed in a digital career but also equip them to navigate the broader world with confidence and adaptability.

🌿 Moving Forward: Continual Learning and Adaptation

The digital world is dynamic and ever-changing, and so too must be your approach to parenting in this space. Stay informed about new trends, tools, and challenges, and be willing to adapt your strategies as needed. The more you learn and grow alongside your teen, the better equipped you'll be to guide them through the complexities of the digital age.

- *Staying Informed:* Make it a habit to stay updated on the latest developments in social media, technology, and digital safety. This might involve reading articles, attending workshops, or simply engaging in ongoing conversations with your teen about their digital experiences.

- *Adapting to Change*: As technology evolves, so too will the challenges and opportunities it presents. Be prepared to adapt your parenting strategies to address new issues as they arise, whether it's a new social media platform, a change in privacy settings, or a new trend that poses risks. Flexibility and openness to change are key to effective digital parenting.

- *Building a Support Network*: Don't hesitate to seek out support from other parents, educators, or digital safety experts. Building a network of resources and people you can turn to for advice and support can help you navigate the challenges of digital parenting more effectively.

- *Continuing the Conversation:* Keep the lines of communication open with your teen as they continue to grow and develop their digital skills. Regularly check in with them about their online experiences, challenges, and successes. This ongoing dialogue will help you stay connected and provide the support they need as they navigate the digital world.

By following the strategies outlined in this book, you can help your teen develop the skills, knowledge, and resilience they need to thrive in the digital age. As a parent, your role is not just to protect them from the potential harms of technology but to empower them to use it as a tool for growth, connection, and positive impact. With the right guidance, your teen can navigate the digital world confidently and responsibly, equipped with the tools they need to succeed in both their online and offline lives.

Thank you for taking the time to invest in your teen's digital future. Your efforts will make a significant difference in helping them become responsible, informed, and empowered digital citizens.